Entrepreneurship After Forty

An Action Plan to Prioritize Your Dream of Financial Freedom

Kris Kendall

Contents

Foreword

When the world shut down in 2020, I was a mom of two high school boys, wife to my high school sweetheart, sister, friend, daughter, best-selling romance author, entrepreneur, and a full-time corporate marketing professional in Silicon Valley.

I had a lot on my plate, and all those roles tugged me in different directions... I loved it!

I absolutely thrive on having fifty balls in the air at once and am always quick to grab a few more. It's just my nature to go, go, go.

So, when all my social circles, volunteer commitments, and work-related engagements disappeared, I had more time on my hands than I ever had before. Not to mention a desperation to keep myself distracted from the scary news that was coming at me from around the world.

That's when I had to make some decisions about what I was going to do next. I was forty-five years old, in a job I enjoyed but had basically "evolved to," and had a yearning to do something that would help others.

See, I'm a doer. A 24/7, never sleeps, always executing the next great idea kinda gal.

When someone mentions a fundraiser for a good cause, I raise my hand to run it. When there's a need for a chaperone or driver for a school event, I adjust my calendar so I can take my multitude of calls from the road or the side of the mountain or from a picnic bench at the zoo. When a friend suggests a girls' trip to Mexico or Vegas or Palm Springs, I'm there. And when my boss mentions new web content or a strawman of an idea, I've got drafts to review by the end of the day.

I rarely slow down, and not being able to connect with people and projects and events during those early months of COVID was torturous.

So, like so many others around the world, I pivoted.

I'd been thinking about exploring a life and business coaching career for years. One of my dearest friends mentioned that I'd been doing it for her and so many others throughout my adulthood, so I might as well get paid for it. It seemed like a perfect fit for what I loved and a way for me to contribute to the success of others.

So when all the other commitments fell off my calendar, I decided to go for it.

And boy, did I ever.

I joined several coaching certification programs and began coaching friends and strangers, honing my skills and crafting my signature program. I evolved and tweaked and switched things up several times in that first year.

My program was almost right...but not quite.

Then, in early 2023, I was introduced to Rachel Rodgers, author of *We Should All Be Millionaires* and CEO of *Hello Seven*. If you're not familiar with Rachel or her company, I'll give you the gist of her business with this simple mission taken right off the Hello Seven website:

Our mission is to help you make more money. *Period*.

We teach you how to increase your income, build wealth, and earn 7 figures per year—without sacrificing your family, health, or sanity in the process.

That was all I needed to know. I was in. One million percent.

I didn't know how or when, but I promised myself that as soon as I had an opportunity to participate in something with Rachel and the Hello Seven team, I would take it.

And, as with all strong and intentional manifestations, not a week passed before I received a response to the waiting list I'd put myself on for her membership program, The Club. But the offer wasn't to join The Club. It was to become a certified coach in Hello Seven's brand-new coaching program.

So I signed up.

It was an easy decision. The framework they use to teach women to MAKE MORE MONEY is in complete alignment with what I've been doing my whole life (literally since I was a change-hustling child) as an entrepreneur and mentor to those ready to make a change and grab that cash.

If you're finally ready to put yourself first and pursue the financial, emotional, and physical fulfillment you've secretly dreamed of but haven't put into action, this book is for you. I'll present the steps I use to guide entrepreneurs through the stages of growth—from the very early ideas for starting a business to earning life-changing profits.

Let's do this, ladies!

Chapter 1

Why Entrepreneurship

As we begin this process of entrepreneurship in our next season of life, we want to start by taking an honest look at what our end goal looks like. Not everyone wants to or needs to be a millionaire. Maybe you just need an extra thousand dollars each month for pocket money. Or maybe a few thousand would allow you to work less and spend more time with your family.

Entrepreneurship isn't always easy, but it's always worth the effort if it's something you care about. So, why do you want to start a business? Is it to make money or maybe to make a difference in the world? Perhaps you're just looking for a fun way to spend your time as you transition out of a high-pressure career. Or do you already have a small business that you want to grow and expand to be your legacy to the world?

For most of us, it's probably a combination of all those reasons that is prompting you to take this next step forward.

Before we dig too deep into the "what" to do, I'd like you to take a moment to think about the "how" you want to do it. If you were to start or expand your business right now, what would that look like 12 months from today? How many hours per day will you be working? Where will you be working? Are you in a location (storefront, office, farmer's market, etc.) outside of your home? Are you sitting in your favorite recliner in front of the TV with your laptop? Have you built a she-shed in your backyard to work from? Imagine the best-case scenario and write down your honest answer to this question:

If everything goes exactly right in your business, where will you be working in a year and how often will you be doing it?

Once you know *when* and *where*, we can think about the *what*.

When you're working, what will you be doing? Are you creating something with your hands? Are you talking to clients? Are you fielding questions from your staff so they can run the business when you're away from your desk? Have you completely outsourced the majority of your business tasks and are only required to make mission-critical decisions while your team takes care of the day-to-day tasks without you?

Visualizing what your business will look like will help you get clarity when you're making decisions about your business. If you're brand-new to entre-preneurship and just starting out with an idea—or maybe you don't even have an idea yet—your answers to those questions might be modest goals.

Maybe you expect to still have a day job, but you'll be working two hours a day on your business after dinner or on the weekends. If you already have a small business and hope to double or triple your profits from where they are today, maybe that means working a lot more hours than you're working now, but only doing the things you do best. Working in your zone of genius while hiring others to do the work you don't love or aren't an expert in.

Documenting this vision of what your business could look like will serve as a constant reminder moving forward. And you're gonna need it! As we take your business from where it is today to five, six, or seven figures over the next 12 months, you will have moments of doubt and fear that might make you want to give up. You might start to believe the little voice in your head that tells you you're not capable of achieving your dreams. You might even forget what those dreams are after facing the challenges that are inevitable with entrepreneurship.

So make your list and keep it handy.

Put it on your phone or as the wallpaper on your computer so you never lose sight of why you're willing to make sacrifices now for what you know will come later.

When I first started my coaching business, I had a few simple goals.

- Earn $10,000 a month from coaching clients
- Earn $20,000 a month from two-day intensives
- Spend ten to twenty hours per week working directly with clients
- Outsource the administrative, accounting, and marketing tasks so I could focus on the work I loved most—helping entrepreneurial women find fulfillment

Although I have other six and seven-figure businesses, I was starting this new coaching practice from scratch. I had no clients, no certifications that meant anything to anyone else, and no network to begin marketing to.

But I did have a day job that I had to juggle my coaching clients around...along with all of my other commitments, my two kids, my husband, my mother who had just moved into my home (permanently, this time), several non-profit boards, and everything else going on.

I definitely wasn't set up for easy success, but most of the time we aren't.

So that's where we'll start with you and your business.

Chapter 2

Your First $50k

If you're starting your business from a baseline of zero, you're in the right place. And if you already have a small business that you want to expand, you're in the right place.

The reason I can say that whether you make zero or $5,000 per month, we'll get your business set up for success and growth, is because every business I've ever worked with has skipped some of the most basic steps for building a strong and sustainable foundation. Those steps are key to scaling your business and helping you achieve the ideal life you just wrote down. By taking a step back and evaluating where you can optimize your effort, you can quickly climb the ranks of revenue generation.

For the sake of this guide, we'll consider the beginning of your business to be one that has not made any money yet or has earned up to $50,000 in revenue (not profits but revenue that may or may not have been reinvested in the business).

To kickstart your journey as either a brand-new entrepreneur or one stuck in the mid-five-figures zone, there are some commonalities among all women, especially as we age and hear more often that we're "too old" to do something new or invest in ourselves.

For example, many of us have a fear of rejection and failure that keeps us from stepping out of our comfort zone. Maybe it's not always there, but it's present in all the wrong moments, maybe even the cause of missing out on some of the best opportunities of our lives.

In my case, I really wanted to go to college on the east coast. I had visions of Wharton or Wellsley or any of the other liberal arts schools in my mind... but I also had a boyfriend who wasn't planning to leave the west coast. And, like many women, I decided to stay for the boy.

Granted, I married him, and we've built an amazing life together, but it just as easily could have gone the other way. Most of my friends who were married young are not still with their spouses...at least not happily, so it's not a path I'd recommend to high schoolers today. But for so many of us, we've been making decisions based on partners, parents, or children's expectations since we were in diapers.

The first half of our life was spent catering to those around us—kids, partners, employers, parents, friends, etc.—and it's easy to forget how to cater to ourselves. We allow the little voices that we've heard for decades to find the cracks in our resolve and worm their way in, holding tight no matter how much we say we want to make a change. They tell us we can't try something new, imagine being bigger and better, or make decisions for ourselves.

We're held hostage by worrying about what our loved ones will think if we say we want to do something they don't believe we're capable of. Or worse, we're worried about what our non-loved ones will think. The people who are always quick to tear us down or point out our problems.

Do you really want to let THOSE people determine how you spend the next phase of your life?

No. Of course not. But you might be inadvertently doing it anyway.

When we allow those little worries to grow into questions, they can be paralyzing and keep most people, but women in particular, from following our dreams and achieving the success inside us.

Questions like:

- What if people hate my idea?
- What if I try to do something...and fail?
- What if I spend money that could go toward retirement, bills, grandkids, car payments, etc...and don't earn it back immediately?

There are so many what-ifs, reasons we *wait*, *research*, *think about*, *consider*, and all the other NON-DOING words you can think of.

All I have to say is...what if they *are* right? What if you do fail? What if you do lose some money? What if there are people who hate your idea?

Then what?

As long as you and your family will still have food on the table and a roof over your heads, is it unthinkable for you to take a gamble on yourself and pursue something that's important to you?

How much money has been spent on sports, art, music, Lego, programming, etc. lessons for your kids that never resulted in a pro career or a paycheck? What about the college degrees that were abandoned after you dumped tens of thousands of dollars on their education? Did those "failures" damage the family or your love for the kids who are now baristas or working in retail or in trades that didn't require any kind of college degree at all? Of course not.

We make choices every day that lead to money gained or lost. And in most cases, life goes on.

Early in our adult life, we usually have less money to spend and more mouths to feed. We can't always prioritize our personal happiness because we're providing for others and making sure many people are happy and healthy...in spite of what it might be doing to our own personal identities.

But as our families grow up and our situations change, so does our relationship with money.

The money we've spent decades earning and saving and investing for everyone else's needs is now available for us to be a little selfish with. If you want to take a trip with your friends, you have the right to do it. If you don't have a lot of disposable income but like to indulge in small pleasures like takeout dinners after work or regular facials, you should be empowered to make those choices without guilt.

And if you decide to pursue a business that will not only set up your own financial security but possibly that of your heirs, you are one thousand percent allowed to do that too.

It's time to look beyond your fear of failure and rejection and remind yourself of all the times other people in your life were given the space and privilege to experiment without the requirement of being successful.

When you put your kid in tumbling class, you probably didn't expect Olympic gold medals. When your kid picked up the guitar or flute or keyboard in middle school, you probably weren't imagining a future concert in Madison Square Garden. You've allowed your family to take chances and try new things because that's how people grow.

And now it's your turn.

Regardless of what other people think, you need to give yourself permission to follow your heart and do the thing you've always wanted to do. Sell the thing, provide the service, or teach the skill that brings you joy.

Not everything will be a breakout success, especially not on day one. But you can still try it.

Try it because you want to.

Try it because it'll make you happy.

Try it because you have the time and money that you've never had in the past.

Try it because *it's finally your time.*

What's the worst that can happen? You might lose some money and time that would have otherwise been spent *waiting, researching, thinking about,* and *considering* what it would be like to start that business of your dreams. If you're like me, you've probably lost money on worse things in your life.

If you do try it and things don't work out, at least you'll know you tried. Whether your next venture is your first or last business, you won't continue to wonder "what could have been." That might be cliche, but that doesn't mean it isn't true.

One of the best ways I've learned to get past this fear of rejection and failure is to acknowledge that you have something to offer the world...and begin to offer it.

Yes, that sounds simplistic, but just the act of telling people you have a product, service, or knowledge that you're willing to sell to them is the first and most crucial step in starting your business.

So what are you going to tell them? We'll talk about that next.

Chapter 3

What Is Your Offer?

Now that you've decided to start or expand your existing business, it's time to create an offer that customers simply can't refuse. In this chapter, we're going to dive into the secrets of crafting an offer that your target audience will want to buy, need to buy, or will buy because they don't want to be the only one not buying it.

If you're brand-new to entrepreneurship, you might not even be familiar with the term "offer." What I'm referring to is the thing you're exchanging for their money. That could be your services. It could be your product. It could be a bundle of services and products that you combine to make a more compelling offer than what others are selling. The options are limitless.

For example, if you sell books, your basic offer might be a book. Or, if you have several books, it might be a box set of all the books in a series for a slightly discounted price than what they would pay if they bought each book individually.

If you're a personal trainer, maybe your offer includes weekly training sessions in the gym of your choice and a T-shirt with your brand on it. As a bonus offer, maybe you'll throw in a nutrition plan to help them reach their goals.

If you make t-shirts, your offer might be three packs of t-shirts or matching shirts for people and their dogs.

Regardless of what you're selling, you need to make your offer stand out from the competition by using language that appeals and resonates with the exact people who want what you have...and compels them to pull out their credit cards.

To make an irresistible offer, you need to anticipate the problems or pain points that your customers might be experiencing and provide a solution. If they are hungry, you provide food. If they are walking in the rain, you provide an umbrella. If they want to play piano, you provide lessons.

People are looking for end results. Put yourself in their shoes and think about why they would say yes to your offer, as well as the reasons they might not be ready to make the purchase.

If they're ready to say yes, stop selling and provide them with a way to pay you. People in sales use the acronym ABC, which stands for "always be closing" [the deal]. When your customer says they're in, it's time to shut your mouth and get paid.

But if they're hesitating or not sure if your offer will fill the need/want/gap they're trying to fill, you need to give them a reason to change their mind. Maybe they're worried about the time commitment or the effectiveness of your service. Maybe they've seen a lower price and want to shop around.

There are countless reasons people give to avoid making a purchase. If you acknowledge their concerns and get them back into the mindset of having the results your offer will provide, you'll build trust and confidence that your offer is the one they should accept.

And by *accept*...I mean buy. With cold, hard cash. That's the goal to keep in mind.

When people buy stuff, it's usually because they're looking for convenience, novelty, or to fill a need. Which of those aspects are you fulfilling? How will you make someone's life more convenient, fun, or easy?

For example, my publishing company provides new authors with services for getting published. It's not unique or something they can't do on their own. Anyone can do it for free if they learn all the steps. But if they don't want to learn it all on their own or don't have the technical prowess to take on new software, they can pay us to do it for them. Some people want the convenience of paying someone to make sure things get done right. I'm selling them ease and convenience. If they want their book published in a few weeks, we offer an option to do it in a painless way.

In order for me to attract people who are looking for that service, I need to prove that my offer provides value. Value that they want or need and consider worth the amount of money I'm charging for it.

Another example is if your service saves people time or money, that savings should be higher than what they'll spend without your offer. If you can teach me how to save $1000, I'd be happy to pay $500 for that knowledge.

It's a win/win. Buying from you should always feel like a win for your customers.

Whether you're selling cupcakes, shoes, or accounting services—the fastest way to get started is to...get started.

We just have to start.

Keep in mind that the first offer you come up with might not be your forever offer. Maybe you start off with cupcakes but realize people keep asking for wedding cakes instead. Or maybe your cat-sitting business evolves into a grooming service. There are no rules when you're starting to build your business. The market will tell you what they want. You just have to be willing to listen.

Offers are meant to ebb and flow with time. What you think people want on day one might not be what they're begging to buy from you on day 50 or 500. Listen to what customers are asking for. They'll tell you what they want from you. And when they do, the ball is in your court. You can choose to meet those requests with variations or customizations of your offer, or you can hold fast to what you love most. Either way, you'll be narrowing your audience to only those looking for what you want to sell.

And the gravy on top is that every bit of feedback you get about your offer is information you will learn and grow from.

I know this might sound intimidating, but it all boils down to the questions, **what do you love doing/making/selling and who is going to pay you for that**? Once you know the answer to those questions, you'll be ready to start selling.

Crafting Your Offer

Once you have an idea of what you want to sell, you need to describe it in a way that clearly articulates what your customer will get and why they should pull out their credit card. A formula I use is to list the pain points your customers are feeling and the solution you have for them.

- Describe the situation they want to change
- Describe how you provide the change they're looking for
- Describe how much better their life will be after using your solution

For example, when I'm talking to aspiring authors about my done-for-you publishing services, this is what I say:

Have you written a book but don't know what to do next? We will take your completed manuscript through all the production stages and upload it to the major retailers so you can hold your very own paperback in just a few weeks. No tech skills required.

It clearly speaks to people who have already written a book and need help with everything that comes after it. I'm not talking to already-published authors, I'm not talking to tech wizards, and I'm not talking to people who want to have their book traditionally published. My ideal audience will read that and say "Yes, that's me. I need that." And everyone else will say, "Not for me." That saves all of us time and resources.

Another example is for a bookkeeping service. They might say something like:

Do numbers make your brain hurt? If balancing your books and keeping track of your profit and loss is the most stressful part of your month, let our team of expert accountants take that off your plate. We'll run the numbers while you focus on what's important - running your business.

That message will resonate with business owners who hate doing their own books. They are looking for a better option and will be happy to see that options exist.

What does that mean for you?

Well, what situation are your customers facing that you can fix? How is your fix going to improve their day/life/health/wealth/marriage etc.? Jot down a few examples for your offer and let them sit for a minute.

Sometimes, when we see the words in black and white, it's easier to find the message that resonates. Again, it doesn't have to be perfect. Keep all your ideas in a document and iterate a "current offer description" at the top of that document. What you love today might not speak to customers the way you think it will. If that happens, you'll have all your previous ideas to pull from to see if maybe a small revision will make a big impact.

Most offers will require testing a few different approaches with your audience until one really lands with them. Maybe your course works better as a group coaching program. Or maybe the group session that you've broken up into twelve weeks of meetings can be combined into a course that can be viewed at the user's own pace. Let your audience help you evolve your offer and messaging until you find the sweet spot of what you love to deliver, what your customers want, and what is most profitable to your business.

Ego has no place in a small business. If you want to provide value to your audience, listen to what they say is valuable.

Chapter 4

Who Are You Selling To

Your ideal audience is the consumer who is most likely to purchase your product. In the Venn diagram of who could use your offer, who wants your offer, who can afford your offer, and who you want to work with, they are the people in the middle.

Your ideal audience isn't "everyone." I hear this more often than you think. If you sell pizza, you might think "everyone" buys pizza. That's not true. If you sell socks, you might think "everyone" buys socks. Also not true. Maybe you sell personal training services, and "everyone" could benefit from a personal trainer. Still not true.

At a high level, you will be tempted to assume that 50% or 80% of the population could use your offer. Maybe that's true, maybe it isn't. But what is true is that there are PERFECT customers for your offer...and identifying who they are and how to reach them is what will determine your success or failure.

Selling donuts outside of a fitness convention is not a sustainable path to success. You might sell a few... but that's not a long-term strategy.

Selling #2 pencils outside of an office building is not the way to make your millions. Sure, a few people might buy one or two, and everyone who passes you could technically use a #2 pencil...but the chances of them having the time to stop, the interest to buy a pencil, and the quarter in their pocket to pay for it are all very slim.

Be smart about where you focus your marketing attention so you not only save money and resources, but more importantly, you find the people who will love what you do, be happy to share it, and will likely know others who also need it.

So, how do you do all that?

Let's start with the obvious audience. You! If you're a perfect customer for your offer, then you can consider people like you as your target audience. But there's likely a bigger audience than "people like you." Also, it's important to understand which of your characteristics make you the ideal customer.

Is it because of your age, your gender, your marital status, the age of your children, whether you own pets, your location, the language you speak at home, your favorite type of entertainment, etc.?

There are so many demographics to consider when defining your target audience, but narrowing down the ones that fit your offer best will make it easier for you to reach them. And when I say "best," I don't mean only. You can sell your offer to anyone who wants it. There will be rogue customers who are unexpected but find you anyway. Consider those to be bonus sales.

In this section, we'll define who the very best prospects are for your offer.

You've already defined what your product is. Now write down who would most benefit from its features, benefits, and the solution it provides.

What are some of the basic demographics you know about the people who are most likely to buy it? What are their age, gender, income level, education, family size, employment status, etc.?

Not all demographics will apply to your offer, so think about the ones that are relevant. For example, if you're selling luxury skincare products, your target audience might be women over the age of 25 who have a high income.

If you're selling sweaters for dogs, your target audience is going to be dog owners with disposable income. But are they more likely to be men or women? What is their age? If you're not sure, it's time to do some market research.

And what if you sell maternity bras? The target audience for maternity bras is probably a woman who is 18 to 35 years old and in her second or third month of pregnancy. Of course, anyone can buy that bra. Friends, partners, parents, and even grandmas of the expectant mom are all possible customers. But instead of marketing to the husband of a pregnant woman who might possibly be thinking about buying her a bra, your messaging and value proposition should be directed at the person who will get THE MOST value from your product. Everyone else (ie. potential customers who aren't your target) is gravy.

In addition to demographics, there are also psycho-graphics. Rather than being physical and objective traits, these are more about the attitudes, interests, personality, values, and lifestyle of your potential customers. For example, if your business is focused on sustainable products, your target audience likely values environmental conservation and reducing waste.

One method of conducting market research is to look at what your competitors are doing and who they're doing it for. Who are their ads targeting? Is it the same audience you want to reach or slightly different? What makes your offer more compelling than theirs and would sway customers to choose yours? These insights into who is interested in offers similar to yours might also identify gaps in the market that you can fill.

If you already have customers or people you've been working with (either paid or free), analyze what their demographics and psychographics are. What are the commonalities between them? Having this as your starting point can provide a strong basis for defining your broader target audience when it comes to marketing your offer.

There is also a lot to be said for old-school research. Surveys, interviews, focus groups, and social media polls will provide valuable insights into consumer preferences and behavior. Having this real feedback from people in your network can help you better understand your target audience.

Creating buyer personas is another method used in the product development and marketing stages of launching products that will come in handy. Once you have information about the different types of buyers who are most ideally suited to hand over their credit card, you can create one or more personas.

Personas are fictional people you make up to represent your ideal customer. In many cases, you'll just have one. But if your product appeals to broader groups, then you might need several personas to help you work out the messaging and marketing channels most appropriate for each audience. Each of your personas will include a combination of demographic details, interests, and behavioral traits and are usually accompanied by a photo (stock image) of this ideal customer. Your personas will help you visualize your customers so you can make informed marketing decisions.

Once you have your audience in mind, you'll want to do some testing to see if your assumptions are valid and the audience you think is ideal...actually is. Marketing is a constant process of trial and error. Which is why you don't need to wait until everything is perfect. Every imperfect launch is an opportunity to gather data and learn more about your offer and your audience. By launching small-scale marketing initiatives, you can test your assumptions and see if the market responds the way you think it should. If it does, you're good. If it doesn't, then adjust your personas until you narrow in on your true target audience.

Market trends and buyer preferences change all the time. As long as you're flexible and willing to pivot to meet the needs of your buyers, you can build a sustainable and profitable business.

Chapter 5

Tell The World You're In Business

Once you've decided on what your business will be and have crafted the outline of your inaugural offer, it's time to start telling people your business exists.

This is your opportunity to showcase your expertise and let the world know what you bring to the table. Don't be bashful about connecting with the network of people you already know because they're your first group of supporters.

Now, I don't mean you should invite them to happy hour at your house and spend two hours trying to sell them housewares or adult toys. I'm talking about a simple announcement to your community of friends, family, colleagues, and acquaintances so they know about your new business.

Of course, not everyone will respond to your offer with a purchase. That's okay. Just because you sell cupcakes and they eat cupcakes, doesn't mean they'll all rush out to buy your cupcakes. But, if anyone you know (or who knows someone you know) is looking for a cupcake baker, they'll know to call you.

Imagine if you wanted someone to paint your house and you had to go online and search through listings of strangers in your city to get bids from random people. It's a painful process full of stress and distrust.

And what if, after you commit to an overpriced company who may or may not do a good job, you find out that your brother-in-law just started a painting company. Wouldn't you have liked to know that before you reached out to strangers? Maybe you would have still gone with a different company, but at least having the information about someone in your network who can provide a service you need is usually helpful when it comes time to make a purchase decision.

So don't be shy about telling people you're in business. I've found that a simple post in my social media and an email to people I have a more personal relationship with can be hugely successful. I'm not asking them to give me money. I'm just letting them know so they can share my contact with anyone who might need it. This kind of low-pressure offer is gold.

Hey there. Hope you're doing well. I just wanted to let you know that I've recently started a business doing xxxxxx, so if you know anyone who might be looking for that, please feel free to send them my way. I'd really appreciate your support as I take on this new venture.

That's it. It doesn't have to be a hard sell, and I've found that if you say "if you know someone" that's less pressure on THEM to respond or buy from you. Maybe they'll also be in the market for what you sell, and that's a bonus if they are, but what you really want is for them to know they can refer you to others. When they're at work or talking to the other parents during soccer practice, if they hear about someone looking to buy what you sell, you want to make sure they know to bring up your name.

Imagine if your close friend was selling something that you really need or want, but they were too afraid to tell you. How would you feel? You'd probably feel a bit hurt or left out of this important milestone in their life.

And if you tell people who aren't supportive or they focus on all the ways your new business can go wrong, those aren't the right people to share this part of your life with. That doesn't mean you have to cut them out of your life, but you can cut them out of the entrepreneurial side of what you're doing. Not everyone will want to see you succeed. Unfortunately, there are always those who want to bring us down so they don't get left behind. Those are the people we leave off the business announcement list, and we just move on in spite of them without their negativity holding us back.

Maybe that ends up being a person close to you, like a spouse, child, or parent. It might hurt your feelings, but keep in mind that they can't control you. You are a grown-ass woman who can make her own decisions. You don't need anyone's permission to follow your passion and dreams. If that means you have to do it quietly and without their support, so be it. There are plenty of networking groups online and in your local community that can be the support system you need if your closest people aren't.

I often hear from new authors that their friends don't want to read their book or their spouse doesn't like their book. My response is that it's okay. Not everyone likes every book. I certainly don't like every book. In fact, the list of book categories I'm willing to read for free is pretty short. If a client is paying me to read their book, I'll read almost anything. But if my neighbor writes something I have no interest in, I'm going to be happy for them and support them in every way possible, but I'm not going to spend three to ten hours of my life reading a book I don't have an interest in.

I don't have time for that, and it's not fair for them to ask me to devote that much of my free time to their project. I might be willing to spend $10 to buy their book as a friend, but if they expect me to read it...that's too big of an ask. I read for PLEA-SURE, and if a book doesn't give me pleasure in the first few minutes, I put it down.

Same with the non-entrepreneurial people in our world. Not everyone has a business owner's mindset. And that's okay. Employees make the world go round. We need them to work for us. But if they can't get behind you and your entrepreneurial aspirations, then don't share it with them. You can talk about all the other stuff in your life, but don't expect them to care about your business if they don't care about your business. Not everyone will.

If you're in that situation, find a support system or network of people who are interested. That might come from an entrepreneurial group on Facebook or with your local Chamber of Commerce. Those are the people who will be excited for your successes and are there to support you during your challenges.

Chapter 6

What Happens If People Respond

Once you start telling people you have a business, be prepared for some of them to want to buy what you're selling. Now, it's not a guarantee that your phone will start ringing off the hook. Depending on how ubiquitous your offer is and how many of the people you initially tell are interested, you might not get any bites.

But if you do get a taker, you need to be ready to not only accept their money...but deliver the promise.

Depending on what you're selling, the product might not even exist yet. Maybe you bake wedding cakes and it's not until after an order comes in and is paid for that the baking begins. But if you're a software consultant and provide a service or you sell products that are expected to be shipped within a few days of the order being placed, you need to be ready to work.

We never want to overpromise and underdeliver. On the contrary, setting conservative timelines and results can lead to over delivering, making sure your customers are delighted by their experience with you and eager to tell their friends about what you did for them.

Don't let the details derail you from taking that first step. At this stage of the game, perfectionism and waiting for everything to be just right is chronic in new entrepreneurs. It's much easier to be *almost* ready and *almost* done and *almost* perfect than it is to just launch and revise as you go.

Because it'll never be perfect.

No matter how much you tweak and adjust and pivot...there will always be "one more thing" you want to do before you put it out in the world.

But it's time to get real with yourself. We're not getting any younger. Every day you wait is one less day you actually have to do it. Whatever "it" is.

When it comes to your first offer, the best you can hope for is deliverable. What I mean by that is you need to know that the thing you're exchanging for money is actually doable. You are capable of providing the product, service, or information that you're selling.

Some of you might be thinking, that's it? We just decide on an offer and an audience and then start selling it? Well, the short answer is yes, that's it. You are ready to be in business without any of that extraneous stuff that usually slows down progress.

But I'll be honest—when I get excited about a new business, all those extra things are the most fun and interesting parts. That's always where I want to start. The website and business cards and logo and color palette and name tags and all the other distractions that keep most of us from ever getting from plan to product.

Which is why I want to encourage you to skip that for now. Not forever. Just at the very beginning.

Depending on your industry and your audience, there is a high likelihood that you can launch with just a conversation and your Venmo account.

Websites are important for established companies, but on day one, everyone will understand if you aren't quite there yet. Besides, until you have a portfolio or collection or more than one offer, there isn't much use for a website anyway. It's just a fancy brochure.

Once you start telling people about your offer, people will begin to show interest by requesting more information or by buying it. All you really need to have ready is an easy and trustworthy method for them to pay you.

For me, that's usually Paypal and Venmo at first, and then I eventually add a payment processor or shopping cart to my website. And really, I do that mostly because I used to be a web designer and still have design clients I make sites for. So, it's just in my nature to start there.

But if your clients aren't going to get new or different information from your website than what you've already told them directly, there isn't any value to devoting your limited resources to building the site up front.

And realistically, depending on what you sell, you might not ever need one.

If your offer is truly in demand, people will be happy to run to an ATM machine on their way to see you or use their kid's Venmo account to get you paid. Don't be stopped up by merchant account drama. Just keep it simple.

Imagine if you met someone who was selling a rare item that you've wanted for a long time. If they offered a great value, would you be offended if they said they only take cash or Venmo? Probably not. If you wanted it bad enough, you'd probably be willing to bust open a piggy bank to get them paid.

Please don't let your fear of details be the reason you can't start telling people about your offer.

What if people don't buy at first?

Once your offer has been shared and people start inquiring about it, they generally fall into two categories.

Buyers or prospects.

If they buy, then you've done the hard part of getting a sale. But for those who aren't ready to buy immediately, the next focus is on nurturing those prospects until they are ready.

Think of these prospects as your first fan club. They will likely become your clients in the future, but they're also advocates for your brand right now.

By staying in front of them and reminding them about who you are and why they became interested in you to begin with, you can build a loyal following of customers.

For most small businesses, your nurturing program will start with a simple email sequence that your prospects enter. You can set up an automation in almost any email program to send out timed messages that start as soon as they join your list.

For example, right when someone subscribes to your mailing list or asks for more information, an email can be triggered. That might be a welcome message or a link to some kind of free information you're providing. This is called a lead magnet because it's used to bring in leads by offering something in exchange for their contact information. Lead magnets are often videos, articles, checklists, worksheets, quizzes or surveys, or downloadable PDFs that are like a teaser to your larger offer.

Once you have people on your mailing list who want to hear from you, you can set up additional emails to go out in predetermined intervals (daily, weekly, monthly, etc.). These emails might be links to blog posts, updates about your products, or just tips and information that's relevant and valuable to your ideal customers.

And in each message you send, be sure there is a clear call-to-action. That's the button or link or action you want the reader to take. Maybe it's a "buy now" button or a link to schedule a meeting with you. Whatever you want them to do should be one of a few specific actions that are easy for your prospects to find so when they make the decision to reach out, they don't have to hunt for a way to do it.

Make it easy for your prospects to become customers.

Chapter 7

Why Money Matters

The early stages of entrepreneurship may seem daunting, especially if you haven't accumulated substantial earnings yet. However, it's all part of the journey you're taking for yourself...and for your legacy. Whether that's children, grandchildren, or charitable organizations you'll eventually leave your estate to, we all want to build as much for our future while we can. The reality is that most of us don't know how long we'll be around, but some of us will still have thirty, forty, or fifty years ahead of us. That's a lot of money we'll need to live comfortably and still leave a little behind.

So, let's talk a bit about the dollars.

When it comes to money, your financial health after forty isn't just a question of what's in the bank —it's about being in command of your fiscal destiny.

Learning how to manage your money and plan strategically for saving and growing it is critical for your business success. It's never too late to become financially literate, and trust me, it's more than crunching numbers and balancing checkbooks.

Think of it this way, when I started out, I barely knew the difference between gross and net income. And when it comes to business finances, you're either a predator or prey. I had to learn quickly that cash flow is the lifeblood of any business, and investment is the fuel for future growth.

Financial Literacy isn't a Luxury. It's a Requirement.

Would you drive a car blindfolded? Of course not. Running a business without understanding money is similarly reckless. Not only do you need to know how to interpret the story behind the numbers but also know how to anticipate challenges and pivot to new strategies as needed.

And financial planning isn't about pinching pennies. I am a spender at heart and never stick to tight budgets that make me limit the things I think are important to growth. But being able to make educated decisions about your business becomes so much easier when you can look at the data and clearly see what's going on.

Being in control of your finances is about making informed decisions, not just about choosing smart investments. And that's after you've created a buffer to withstand financial hardships that inevitably come up in your life and your business.

I've seen too many brilliant minds lose their businesses to unexpected circumstances because they lacked an emergency fund or didn't have diverse revenue streams that could keep them afloat for a while.

By understanding where every dollar goes, and more importantly, where it can work for you, you can shield against economic volatility and be ready to take advantage of beneficial opportunities when they arise.

We often talk about stability as if it's the end goal, but it's just the beginning. Achieving stability is the launch pad for innovation. It's where risk becomes calculated and dreams transform into executable plans that can catapult your small business.

Having the freedom to experiment, to grow, and to explore untapped markets might sound grandiose, but in business, thinking big is just as important as acting cautiously. As an entrepreneur, your experience and wisdom is your edge, and stability is what allows you to wield it effectively.

Mastering financial literacy is an ongoing journey. Markets evolve, new financial tools emerge, and business models change overnight.

Staying on top of your money is not optional.

Navigating the entrepreneurial waters in midlife is daunting, but you've got the experience and the tenacity to be successful. Now it's time to arm yourself with cutting-edge financial strategies to ensure you get there.

Understanding your financial well-being involves an honest assessment of your current financial situation. Take an inventory of your assets, liabilities, income, and expenses. This comprehensive understanding of your finances will help you create a strategic plan to achieve your financial goals.

Then look at where the bulk of your revenue is coming from. Are there a few products that make 90% of your revenue? Or maybe one product does the heavy lifting, and everything else either costs you money or is completely ignored by your audience. Being honest about what your customers want is the best way to streamline your offer and focus on the moneymakers.

It can be hard to eliminate products that don't serve you or your customers, but data is data. And whether you act on it is up to you, but having the information is the first step to leveling up your business.

Every decision you make now will impact the future of your business and your finances. Don't underestimate the power of informed decision-making.

You have the power to take control of your financial well-being and set yourself up for success in the years to come.

Chapter 8

Let's Do This

We've talked about everything you need to get started. Now it's up to you. I can't do it for you, but if you're serious about taking the next steps toward building a business that will secure this next stage of your life, I can help you.

Whether you want weekly coaching sessions to keep yourself accountable for your goals and help making decisions when you're at a crossroads, or you want to book an intensive weekend to just buckle down and get it all set up over 48 hours in the city of your choice, we can do this together.

My entire business is built to help women like you who are ready to start and grow a business. I can help you at every stage, from concept and strategy to marketing and setting up business systems.

You don't have to do this yourself. Not only will a business coach be your biggest champion and most honest critic, but I'll help you connect with a squad of supporters who you can reach out to when you need a shoulder to cry on, a sounding board for ideas, or a cheering squad to celebrate your successes.

I'm so proud of you for getting this far in the journey of entrepreneurship after forty. Let's keep this forward momentum going and get you to six, seven, or eight figures over the next 12 months.

It's possible if you want it. You just have to put yourself first and prioritize your dreams!

About the Author

 Kris spent the first half of her life working in Silicon Valley for large and small companies, building marketing programs to grow them to billion-dollar enterprises. And then she realized she had dreams of her own.

Now, she enables women over forty to identify and pursue their passions and interests to create a second half of their lives that brings fulfillment and joy.

As a prolific romance author, mother, sister, wife, daughter, and best friend to many, she can relate and empathize with everything you're going through and help you emerge even stronger and better on the other side. She's also the managing editor at Surrendered Press, offering Author Coaching and Done-For-You services for new and aspiring authors.

Fulfilled After Forty: https://www.fulfilledafterforty.com/

Discounted rate for readers for the "2 months of progress in 2 days" intensive: https://www.fulfilledafterforty.com/intensive

fulfilledafter40@gmail.com

facebook.com/fulfilledafter40

instagram.com/fulfilledafter40

youtube.com/@FulfilledAfterForty